CONTENTS

What is a Shark?

The menacing triangular fin of a circling shark is a fearsome sight.

When most of us think of sharks, we picture fearsome man-eaters. Sharks are the most feared creatures in the sea, but most are not as menacing as the great white shark, a notorious man-eater. Some sharks don't grow much longer than 30 centimetres, and a number of the biggest are completely harmless. Some are regularly eaten by humans.

All sharks are fish. But they are different from other fish. They have no bones, no gill covers, no scales, and no swim bladders. Instead of bone, they have cartilage. Cartilage is the flexible gristle that most animals have at their joints. Sharks belong to the group known as cartilaginous fish, or

Chondrichthyes. Skates and rays also belong to this group.

Instead of gill covers, sharks have simple slits which open and close to allow water to flow out. Instead of swim bladders to keep them afloat, they have large livers, rich in oil, which is lighter than water and helps keep the shark buoyant. And instead of scales on their skin, they have tooth-like growths called *denticles*, which act as both a weapon and a defensive armour.

Sharks were once thought to be primitive fish, with small brains and poor senses. We now know that they are complex and sophisticated animals.

The silvertip is a typical medium-sized shark. It grows to about 3 metres in length and lives in the Red Sea and the coral reefs of the Pacific Ocean.

Remora, or shark sucker

SKIN OF A SHARK

Shark skin is covered with thousands of sharp denticles, which make the skin rough. It was once used as sandpaper.

Shark Ancestors

Fossilized sharks' teeth help to determine when sharks first appeared.

SHARKS are among the oldest creatures alive today. When the dinosaurs first appeared on earth, about 225 million years ago, sharks had already been here for 175 million years. Humans are newcomers by comparison. The first recognizable human ancestor, *Australopithecus*, emerged only five million years ago.

However, although there is some evidence of the existence of early shark-like fish from fossils of their teeth, it is not known for certain when sharks first appeared in the world's oceans. Sharks may have evolved from a group of fish known as *placoderms*, which are now extinct. Placoderms had shark-like jaws and were covered in an armour of large, bony plates.

Another possibility is that both sharks and placoderms descended from an unknown common ancestor which lived during the Silurian period, 390 million years ago.

Silurian	*Devonian*	*Carboniferous*	*Permian*
390 m years	*350 m years*	*300 m years*	*215 m years*

Ancestors

Cladoselache

Goodrichthys

Hybodus

The Hybodonts, (such as *Hybodus* and *Goodrichthys*), took over from *Cladoselache*, which died out 225 million years ago.

The first evidence of fish that could really be described as sharks was found in rocks that date from the Devonian period, 350 million years ago. These fish, known as *Cladoselache*, were about 108 metres long. Their bodies and fins appear very similar to those of modern sharks, but it is not certain that they are direct ancestors. The first modern sharks appeared in the Cretaceous period.

The time chart (BELOW), *divided into geological ages, shows how long sharks have lived on earth.*

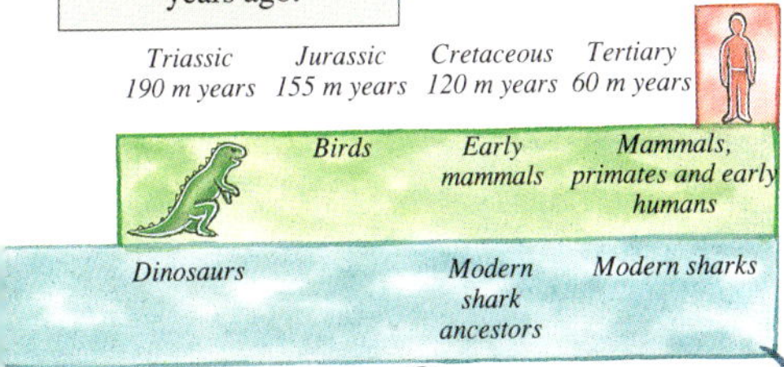

WHERE DO SHARKS LIVE?

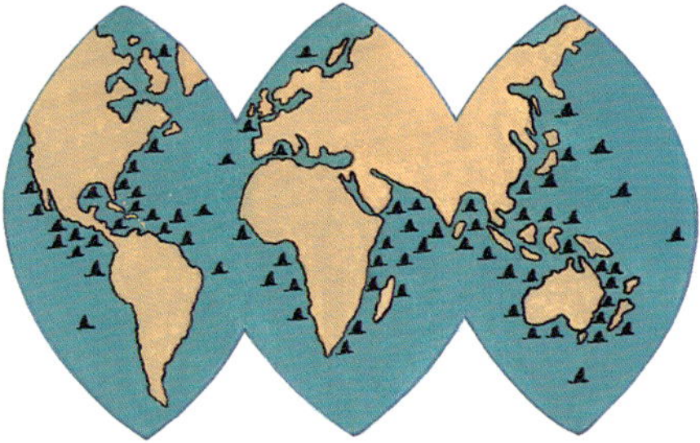

THERE are sharks in all the world's oceans. Sharks also live in different ocean depths. They have been caught in water as deep as 3,500 metres. Deep-water sharks, such as the angel shark, that live on or near the ocean floor have flat bodies, like skates and rays. Species such as the cookiecutter shark are known to rise more than seven kilometres from the ocean floor, where they spend the day, to the ocean's surface, where they feed at night. Basking sharks spend most of their time on or just

Sharks have established themselves worldwide. The fins on the map (ABOVE) *show where sharks have been found. Sharks of some kind live in every ocean, from the Arctic to the tropics, in coastal waters and far out to sea. However, most shark species live in warm waters.*

below the surface. They live far away from land, and swim slowly with their mouths open to catch plankton. Nursing sharks live in the reefs of shallow tropical waters. Hammerhead sharks also live in shallow tropical waters.

Sharks are also found in lakes and rivers. The bull shark is the most common freshwater shark, but there is another variety, the Ganges shark. This rare shark is named after the river where it is found, but little else is known about it.

Freshwater Sharks

Not all sharks live in the sea. The bull shark is the commonest freshwater member of the shark family. It is found in lakes and rivers, including the Mississippi, Amazon, Ganges, and Zambezi. Bull sharks have been found far up the Amazon River, over 3,000 kilometres from the coast.

Many sharks live in the shallows where food is plentiful. Hunters prefer the mid-depths of the open sea. Slow swimmers trawl the ocean depths.

How Big are Sharks?

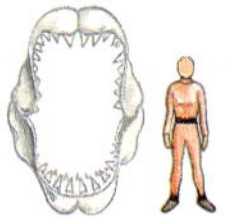

Megalodon was a shark that lived 12,000 years ago. Its jaw measured 1.8 metres across.

SHARKS come in all sizes. Although there are about 350 species of sharks, only 40 species are known to grow more than three metres in length. More than half of all known species never reach more than one metre in length.

The smallest species of shark is the appropriately named dwarf shark. Fully-grown adult dwarf sharks measure only 15 centimetres in length and weigh less than 30 grams. Another pocket-sized shark is the spined pygmy shark, which grows to about 25 centimetres in length.

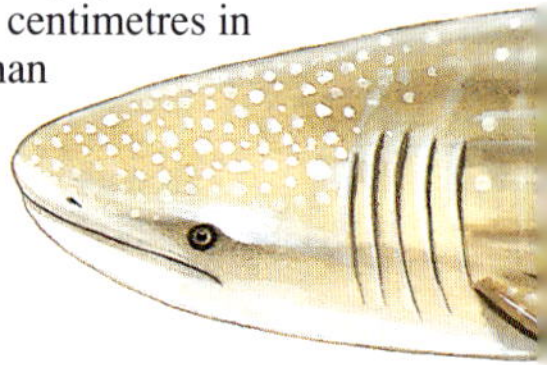

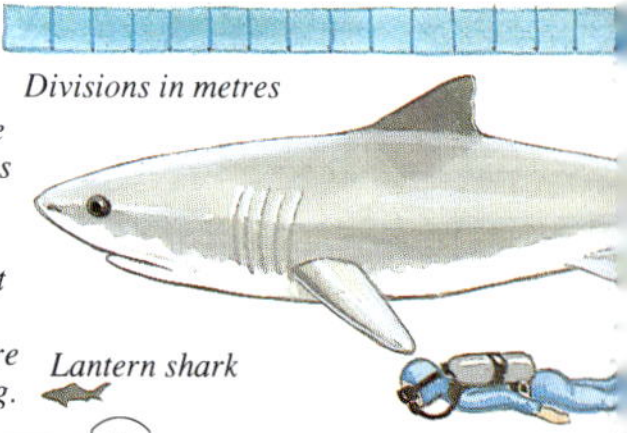

Whale sharks are the world's largest fish. One whale shark can weigh as much as two African elephants. The longest great white shark caught so far measured nine metres. Lantern sharks are about 20 centimetres long.

At the other end of the scale, the largest shark is the whale shark. This is the largest fish in the world, and can grow as long as 18 or 20 metres. The next largest shark is the basking shark, which can grow to 12 metres or more in length.

Although they are enormous, both the whale shark and the basking shark are quite harmless. They feed only on plankton and very small sea animals. The largest of the dangerous species is the great white shark, which grows to about six or nine metres.

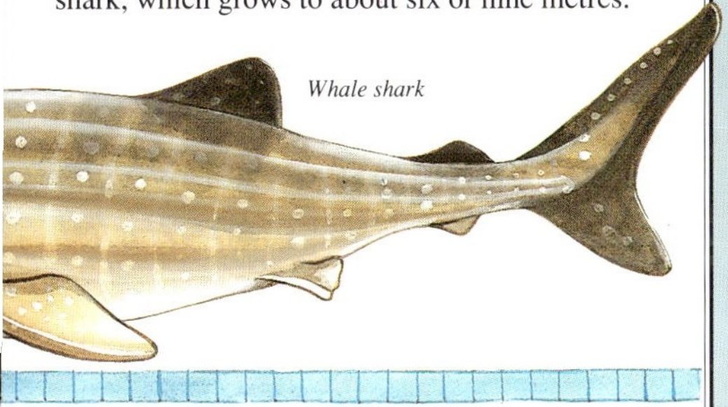

Whale shark

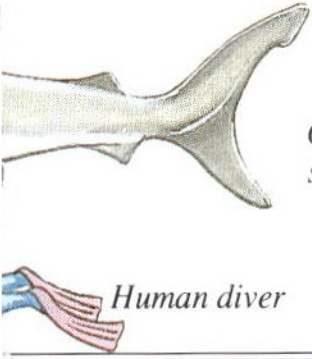

Great white shark

Human diver

GREAT WHITE GIANT

The heaviest great white shark on record weighed 3,300 kilograms and was 6.4 metres long.

Shark Anatomy

Shark skeletons are made of flexible cartilage, which means that sharks can twist and turn to hang on to struggling prey.

Most shark species have long, cigar-shaped bodies that are well adapted to glide effortlessly through the water. The shark propels its sleek body through the depths by the powerful movements of its tail. Its tail is crescent-shaped, with the upper part larger than the lower. This design gives lift to the tail,

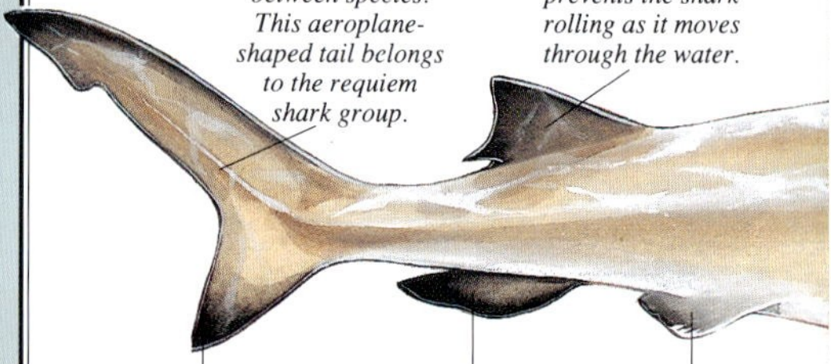

Rich Liver

Sharks have large oil-rich livers. The oil is lighter than water and helps to keep the shark afloat. Sharks were once hunted for this oil, which is a rich source of vitamin A, and was used to make candles and lamp oil.

helping to compensate for the shark's weight.

To change direction, the shark uses its *pectoral* fins, which jut out from behind the fish's head on either side. Two more side fins, lower down the body, help to lift the front part of the shark and keep it balanced.

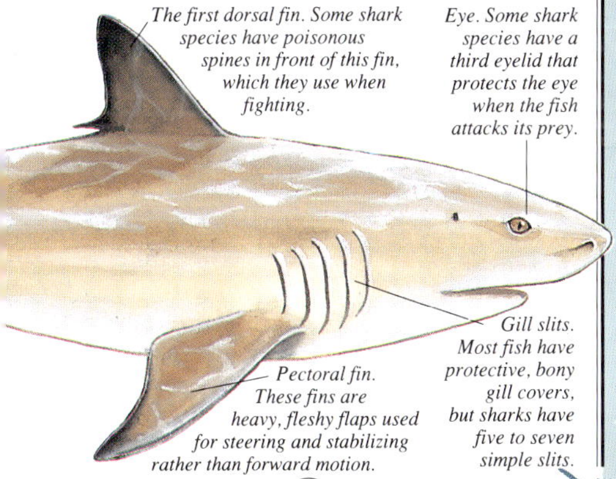

JAWS AND TEETH

THE shark is a hunter and a meat-eater – its teeth are its main weapon. Most shark species have teeth designed to pierce, stab, cut, and tear, and so they are triangular in shape, with sharp points and razor-like edges. There are variations on this basic design. Porbeagles have two additional, small, sharp points, or cusps, at the base of each tooth.

Sharks that eat crabs, lobsters, and molluscs, such as the smooth hound sharks, have flat teeth arranged in regular rows which are used to crush and grind the shells of their prey.

JAW PRESSURE

Sharks' teeth are powered by their jaws. The dusky shark, which is about 1.8 metres long, has a biting pressure of 3.3 tonnes per square centimetre.

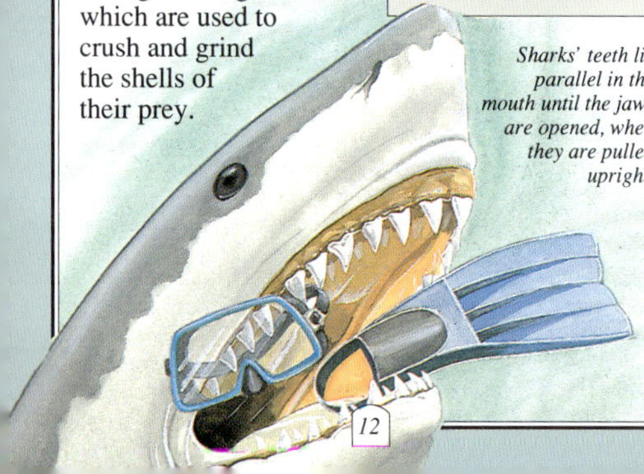

Sharks' teeth lie parallel in the mouth until the jaws are opened, when they are pulled upright.

Teeth Shapes

Most large sharks, including the man-eaters, have sharp, pointed teeth with saw-like edges, which slice through the flesh of their prey.

Some sharks have long, thin teeth which skewer prey and prevent it from wriggling away.

Some sharks have grinding teeth, like human molars, which crush their prey.

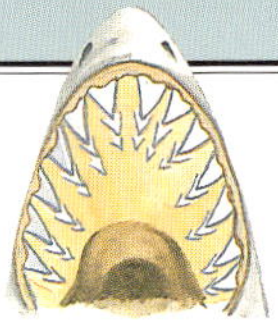

Renewable teeth

Whatever kind of teeth the shark has, they are arranged in the same way, on a kind of conveyor belt that makes certain the shark will never be toothless. The teeth are arranged in rows. If a tooth wears out, or is destroyed and falls out, the tooth behind it moves forward to take its place. Replacement teeth lie out of sight, along the inside of the shark's jaws.

In one year, a shark might chew its way through a few thousand new teeth. As young sharks grow older, their teeth grow bigger, to deal with larger prey.

Senses and Special Organs

Sharks are at the top of the ocean food chain. Their only predators are other sharks, and people. Besides their fearsome teeth and flexible bodies, sharks have other keen senses and special organs to help them stay on top.

Sharks have a very good sense of smell. Almost two-thirds of their brain is used in decoding scent messages. They can also hear well. It was once thought that sharks could not see well, but this is not the case. Although they cannot see close-up details clearly, they can spot prey in clear water from 15 metres away. Porbeagles may even be able to see in colour. They have colour receptors on the retina at the back of their eyes.

Brain Size

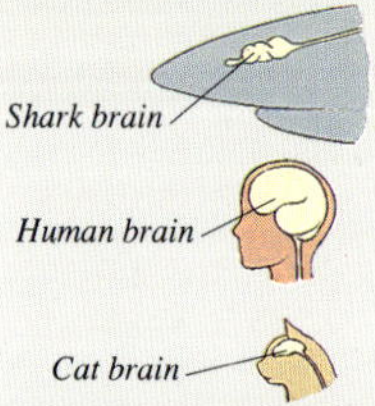

Scientists once thought that sharks had primitive, small brains. Now it is known that the shark's brain is larger in comparison to its body size than that of most fish, some birds, and some mammals. Recent studies have even found that some species of shark are able to learn tasks, such as pressing a lever to obtain food.

Sharks have their own version of radar, which operates from special organs in their snouts.

In their snouts, sharks have special organs called the *ampullae of Lorenzini*. These are deep pores, filled with waxy jelly, and connected to nerve cells at the base. Hunting sharks, such as the hammerhead shark, have many ampullae.

Like radar receivers, the ampullae are sensitive to weak electrical signals from other living things and metal objects. The information from these signals is used by the shark to detect and attack prey, and to understand its surroundings.

KEEP ON SWIMMING

Even when they are asleep, sharks have to keep on the move. They are unable to pump water over their gills to obtain oxygen, and so they must keep the water flowing through their mouths and over their gills by constantly swimming. An exception is the *nurse shark*, which can pump water over its gills, and often lies motionless on the sea bottom.

BIRTH AND DEATH

SHARKS have long lives. In the wild, sharks may live between 20 and 40 years. The spiked dogfish, the most common of sharks, has the longest recorded lifespan – 40 years. Scientists believe that these sharks can live for up to 100 years. The great white shark may also reach this grand old age.

Unlike some other wild creatures, sharks live no longer in captivity than in the wild. Several scientific projects are underway to tag sharks and re-release them into the ocean to learn more about their habits, needs, and lifespans.

Sharks also have long gestation periods – the time in which they develop in the egg or the female shark's uterus. For example, spurdog young spend up to 22 months

The chart (BELOW) compares the lifespan of various animals, taking the human lifespan to be 70 years.

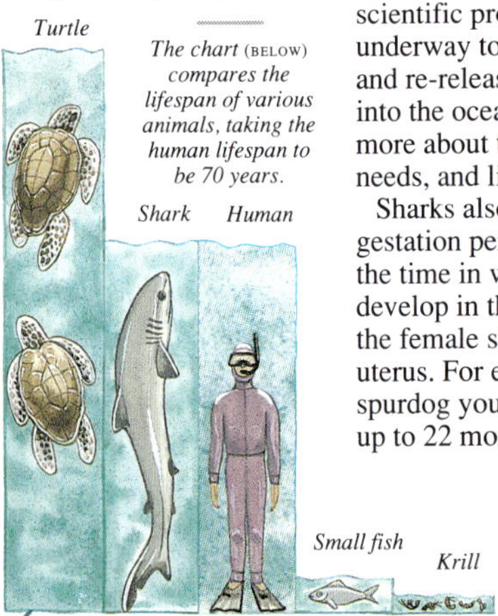

developing – one of the longest gestation periods in the animal world.

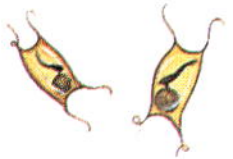

Dogfish egg-cases are often found entangled in seaweed. They are also known as mermaid's purses.

Sharks have different methods of reproduction. Some, like the dogfish, lay eggs. These eggs are individually packed into oblong sacs which are attached to seaweed by tendrils. In other species, such as the spurdog, the eggs hatch inside the female. The young are born live, trailing the yolk sac which will be their food supply for the first few days of life. Other sharks, such as the blue shark, give birth to live young just as mammals do. Before they are born, the pups eat the unfertilized eggs inside their mother to nourish them for life outside.

Live-born shark pups are exact, tiny replicas of their parents.

As soon as young sharks are born, they have to fend for themselves. There is no such thing as parental care in the shark world. Adult sharks are the greatest predators on young sharks.

SMALL FRY

Shark young are called *pups* and are born in *litters*. Most shark litters are quite small, usually between five and ten pups. Larger species may have up to 60 pups at a time.

FOOD FOR SHARKS

Sharks eat anything that can be found in the ocean. Everything from old tin cans to human remains have been found inside these swimming, eating machines.

SHARKS live to eat. There are no shark social units, no time is spent caring for the young, and no time is wasted hiding from predators. Most of a shark's life is spent in the search for food, and their bodies are very well adapted for the hunt. If they cannot find food for a long time, the vitamin-rich oil in their livers keeps them going for weeks.

Except for the whale shark, which lives on plankton, and the basking shark, which eats very small sea creatures and plankton, sharks eat meat. That means fish of all species, including other sharks.

Mackerel sharks, including the porbeagles, great white sharks, and mako sharks, are so named because they eat shoaling fish such as mackerels, pilchards, herring, and anchovies. Great white sharks take larger prey, such as tuna, sea lions, and other sharks. Blue sharks also eat

Sometimes, when sharks of various species gather around a large prey, such as an injured whale, the sharks go into a feeding frenzy. Suddenly, they begin to swim very fast and erratically. As they become more excited, the sharks bite anything they come across, even other sharks and parts of their own bodies. The frenzy of tumbling bodies in blood-clouded water continues for seconds or minutes. Then just as suddenly, the sharks stop threshing about, and those that still can, swim away.

mackerel and pilchards, and often raid fishing nets. Sharks also eat whiting, cod, rays and skates, crabs, lobsters, sea urchins, shrimps, and molluscs. Dogfish add sand eels, worms, and squid to their diet. But this menu is not final. Sharks will eat whatever they find.

IN FOR THE KILL

SOME species of shark, such as topes and smooth hounds, hunt in packs, but most sharks hunt alone.

With their sharp teeth and their rough skin, sharks are well armed for the hunt. A brush from the shark's skin is enough to leave a bleeding wound on any prey animal.

Sharks cruise along at five to seven kilometres per hour on the lookout for prey. They first detect it by smell. They can sniff out a few drops of blood from 450 metres away.

Sound waves in the water also attract the shark's attention. Like other fish, sharks have lateral lines

When the shark bites its prey, its hinged jaws open very wide, bringing its mouth up from the underside of its head.

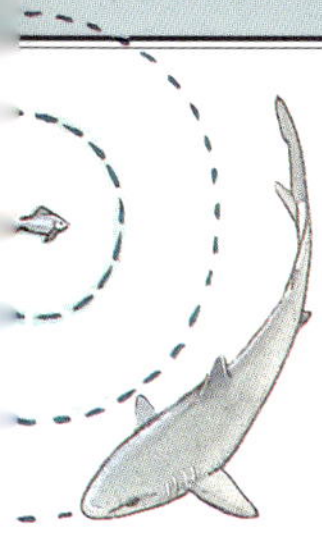

Attracted by smell and sound waves, the shark circles its prey as it comes in for the kill.

along the sides of their bodies which can pick up even small changes in water movements, such as those that an injured fish or a struggling swimmer might create. Sharks can detect movement from 90 metres away.

When it locates its prey, the shark's body stiffens and it begins to swim faster, threshing with its tail. Then it circles in, using its vision and the special organ in its snout to guide it. As it makes its final pass for a bite on its prey, the shark arches its back and opens its jaws. If the shark bites into large prey, such as a whale, a sea lion, or a human, it will roll over repeatedly, tearing the victim to pieces.

Fast Mover

Sharks move quickly when hunting. A blue shark has been recorded travelling at 70 kilometres per hour.

SHARKS AND HUMANS

WHILE just about anything in the water is open to attack by sharks, the sharks' only real enemy is man. All over the world, humans have been killing sharks for centuries. Millions of sharks have been killed for food, for their skin, for oil, or simply to protect beaches. Sport fishermen pursue active species such as the mako shark, which leaps out of the water when hooked on a fishing line and provides an exciting struggle. Unfortunately, some fishermen cut off the dorsal fin as a trophy and throw the shark back into the sea where it soon dies.

However, humans have always feared and respected sharks. Many cultures have developed elaborate rituals around them. Natives of some of the Solomon Islands toss young pigs into the reef waters around their islands as offerings to the

The shark fishers of Papua New Guinea call sharks to their fishing boats using rattles made from coconut shells. Then they trap a shark in a noose and club it to death.

Helping Out

Human beings are trying to overcome their fear of sharks. Many scientists now explore the shark's world to observe shark behaviour, even assisting at a difficult birth. Lemon sharks are much studied as they are small enough for humans to deal with and easily captured when they swim into the shallows to give birth.

sharks. The Solomon Islanders hope that this will prevent the sharks from attacking fishermen. The pearl divers of Sri Lanka, who work among sharks, successfully chase off any which try to attack by shouting at them underwater. And on some of the islands of Fiji, fishermen kiss the bellies of sharks they have captured. They believe it will protect them from attack on future fishing trips.

Fear and Fascination

The sharkmobile. Corvettes customized to look like mako sharks found a ready market in California.

EVEN people who rarely go into the water shiver a little when they read or hear about a shark attack. But, much as most of us fear sharks, there is very little chance of ever being attacked. Each year, fewer than 100 humans are attacked, and more than two-thirds of those attacked survive. Dogs are more of a threat to humans than sharks. Three million people are bitten by dogs every year, although only about a dozen are killed. Most people who run into sharks in the water generally come away without injury.

Protecting the Beaches

People have tried many methods of protecting beaches from shark attack. None of them have worked very well. People have created walls of air bubbles and installed underwater electrical wires which give a weak shock if touched. So far, the most effective methods are netted areas for swimming and cages for divers.

Sharks may attack cages in mistake for prey because they have picked up magnetic signals from the metal.'

None of these statistics stop people from worrying about being attacked by sharks. Shark attack is a universal fear, which affects even people who live nowhere near the sea. At the same time, most people are fascinated by the idea of a big, powerful hunter silently patrolling the ocean. That is why the film *Jaws* was so popular.

Just when you thought it was safe ... Jaws *thrilled and fascinated millions of filmgoers.*

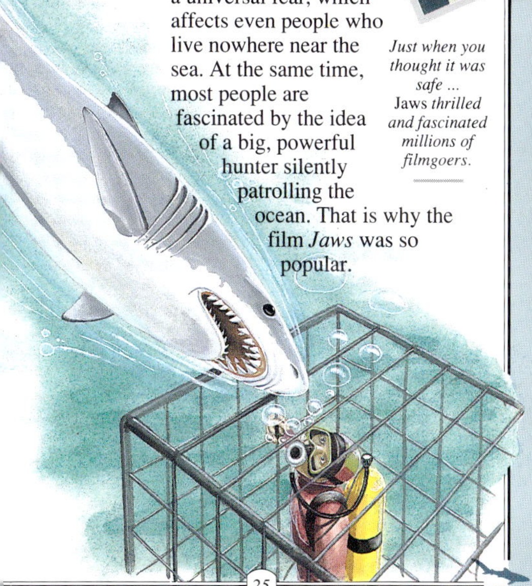

Sharing the Ocean

Sharks have been known to attack humans, to raid fishing nets, and even to turn on small fishing boats, but that does not mean that we should not share the ocean with these magnificent, powerful fish.

Remember that sharks do not attack out of cruelty, but because they are looking for food or have been disturbed or injured by humans. The worst shark attack in the United States occurred in 1916 in the waters off New Jersey. In just 10 days, four people were killed and one was severely injured. All-out war was declared on sharks throughout the New Jersey area, and many were killed by guns, spears, nets, and even dynamite. Eventually a great white shark 2.5 metres long was captured. A human shin and rib

The shark's eye view of swimmers.

were found in its stomach, but it is unlikely that a single shark was responsible for all the attacks. Remember that in the ocean, the shark is king. Even with all our modern equipment, we are still strangers in the world where the shark rules.

Golden Rules

If you are swimming in waters where there are sharks, follow the guidelines provided by the Shark Research Panel to keep yourself safe.

1) Never swim alone.
2) Never swim with an open wound, as blood attracts sharks.
3) Never swim at night.
4) Never swim in dirty water, where you will not be able to see a shark approaching.
5) If a shark is sighted, leave the water immediately.
6) Swim as smoothly as possible; sharks are attracted by threshing movements.
7) Never grab hold of a shark, even an apparently harmless one.

Where Sharks Attack

THERE are about 350 species of shark, but only two dozen species are reported to have been involved in attacks on humans.

Australia has more shark attacks than any other place in the world. Of the 319 recorded Australian attacks, 220 have been along the east coast. This is where most of the swimming and surfing beaches are found. Evidence suggests that sharks are attracted by the noise and movement of people in the sea. From the shark's underwater viewpoint, a surfboard looks like the outline of a seal, one of the shark's favourite prey.

The United States has the second-most attacks. The US Navy Shark Attack File records 225 attacks in the US, three-quarters of them on the east coast. Almost half the world's attacks by great white sharks happened on a 200-kilometre section of the California coast.

Most attacks occur in the shark belt between the latitudes of 47°S and 46°N.

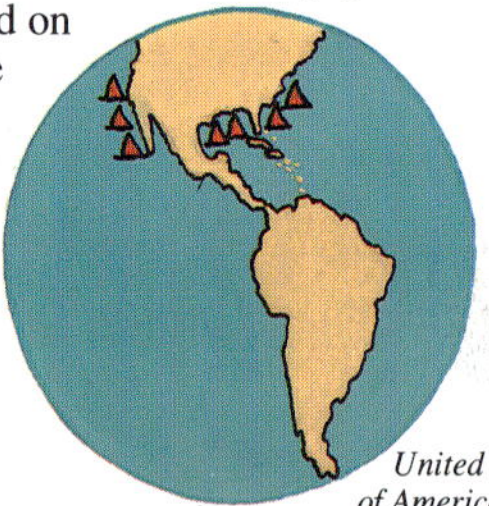

United States of America

THE MAN-EATERS

Bull shark

Tiger shark

Great white shark

The sharks who carried out the most recorded attacks are the great white, the tiger, and the bull.

Europe has seen few attacks, but many of the dangerous shark species live in European waters and two-thirds of the attacks in Europe have had fatal results – a higher proportion than anywhere else in the world.

The Persian Gulf, the Ganges Delta in India, and the coastline of Bangladesh have also had a high number of shark attacks. Attacks have also been recorded around Japan and South America.

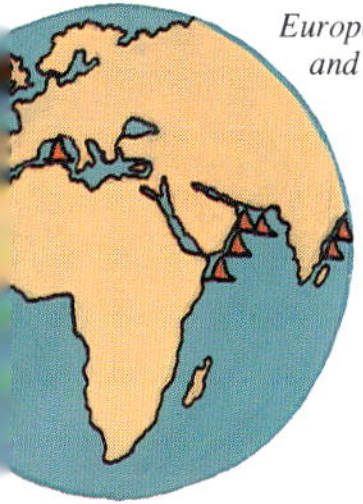
Europe and India

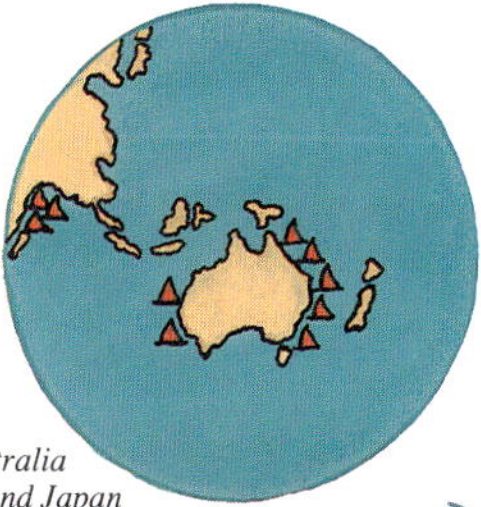
Australia and Japan

CONSERVATION

NOT too long ago, we thought of the ocean as a limitless resource. There could be no end to the creatures that live in such vast waters. We could take all the fish we wanted, for food, manufacturing, or sport, and the ocean would simply replace what we had taken.

Today, we know that over-harvesting and pollution have taken a heavier toll than anyone dreamed possible. Not only have we taken much more from the oceans than we should have, but we have used their waters as a giant sewer.

Sharks are as affected by human activity in the ocean as any other fish.

Many sport fishermen are now practising catch-and-release fishing. When the fish is caught, it is weighed, tagged, and often photographed – and then returned to the water alive.

THE UNFOLDING WORLD

THE FOLD-OUT PANORAMA

The fold-out panoramic chart opposite shows a representation of an ocean full of sharks. Of course, not all sharks appear in the same waters, and so the sharks shown here will not always swim together. Since there are 350 species of shark, not every one can be shown.
The sharks illustrated here have been chosen to show how various species feed and behave in different areas and depths of the seas.

How to Help

You can help to save the sharks in several ways.

Refuse to buy any product that has been made using shark. For example, avoid restaurants that serve shark's fin soup, or write to companies that manufacture it expressing your concern.

Check with your local library or university marine biology department for the latest information about the plight of sharks. Keep yourself, your family, and your friends informed.

Write to your MP and ask him or her to include sharks whenever protection is considered for other species.

We are killing the sharks faster than they can replace themselves – sharks produce new generations much more slowly than other species. In addition, we are destroying their habitats and killing the species that they feed on. However, scientists are working to find out more about sharks, and for most species there is still hope. But they will need careful attention, and some help from legislation, which may not come into effect for some years.